# FULL CATASTROPHE LIVING

*Winner of the Iowa Poetry Prize*

# FULL

# CATASTROPHE

# LIVING

## ZACH SAVICH

UNIVERSITY OF IOWA PRESS

IOWA CITY

University of Iowa Press, Iowa City 52242
Copyright © 2009 by Zach Savich
www.uiowapress.org
Printed in the United States of America

Design by Richard Hendel

The University of Iowa Press is a member of Green Press
Initiative and is committed to preserving natural resources.

Printed on acid-free paper

ISBN-13: 978-1-58729-798-4
ISBN-10: 1-58729-798-1
LCCN: 2008935532

09  10  11  12  13  P  5  4  3  2  1

FOR MEG SCHÄFER

# CONTENTS

## ACKNOWLEDGMENTS

I'm grateful to the editors of these journals, who first published the following poems:

"Movie," *Mid-American Review;* "Outside Santa Maria in Trastevere," *Kenyon Review;* "Serenade," *American Letters and Commentary;* "Countryside," *New Ohio Review;* "Animal," *Natural Bridge;* "On a Pose of Virgil's," *Iowa Review;* "Then . . . ," "Why Lie," and "View from Above and Below," *Cranky;* "Reconsidered Vitamins," *88;* "For You to Find You Love Me, and Tell Me So," *Laurel Review.*

Portions of "Fool," sometimes in earlier forms, appeared in *Forklift, Filter, La Fovea, Iowa Review* (reprinted by *The Daily Palette*), *Turbine,* and *580 Split.* The complete "Fool" appeared as a chapbook commemorating my reading with Mark Leidner at the Exploding Swan reading series in St. Louis. Mark Strand selected "On a Pose of Virgil's" for inclusion in the anthology *Best New Poets 2008.*

# FULL CATASTROPHE LIVING

Now the cardboard orange juice carton
dissolves in rain

You: I can never say *tread* without hearing *tremble*

Or *lovely* without *cold*

So they hitched the farmhouse to a rig
like a tooth to a doorknob

You: I feel the same

I argued first what's the point—the cabinets
and floorboards and curtains the same

Then countered I wouldn't mind if only my body
moved, was moved

I can never say *fervent* without
hearing *furtive*

Stalks bent in snow like lavender in soap

Or a night running home in lightning I
saw my shadow, headless,
on the shoulder-high corn

Corn in the gravel like gulls on a shore

You: There is still the problem of attraction

Now we are leaving the theater early

Now we are driving to where the house was

You stand where it was

You: You watch me stand where it was

That the valved

values

a studied pause,

steadying

a lengthening

perspective the eye

runs along,

as a gate's latch

fallen to—

beauty so consoled,

and consequent,

you turn away

A tight curve I

    drive through

as the art is

    out of our hands

one's lotioned

    lotioning

look to me

    like a house with no

windows on the wind-

    side

IN BED. Don Quixote at the edge of the stage
and the play is about Don Quixote.
Don Quixote in the audience.
The seat flips up
when Don Quixote leaves at intermission,
purchases a small plate
of assorted finger cakes
and does not return;
the play is even more about Don Quixote.
I write it with an *x* still, not a *j*. X,
a kiss, my signature.
Put her there.
*Kissing*, I yell at the photographers
and kiss whoever is at hand, e.g.,
the x on my hand meaning I am inside.
YOURS, WITH HELL.
A student is watching from the window of the school.
I first wrote *of the scar.*
I tell the student, privately,
we are in Hell. Because then, everything is logical.
I drink the coffee, avoiding the snow.
Would you like me to warm you up?
All the signs say stop.
The snow is falling, and I am falling.
I pull out the stitches like I'm trying to start something.
ON STAGE. On stage: sunset, yellow
as a subway platform's line. One steps past,
blindfolded, and falls erotically to the audience.
I.e.: head wrapped in mini-blinds?
To use *tilt* as a verb is to refer to Don Quixote.
I tilt sincerely at the crocus, and the crocus is a windmill.
I've read about things like this.
Every sentence ending, I hope.
It has at least multiple meanings.
If you pushed a flowerpot from the sill, I'd wear it as a hat.
HOW DO PRIESTS EXERCISE THEIR STOMACHS?
It is not that breath holds up the feather,
but that *feather* is a metaphor for breathing;

thirty chest compressions for each two breaths
   is the new method of revival.
I whittled the hose rubber from the frozen spiral of water.
   Then stood in its center: Saturn.
      I tacked blankets to the windows for heat,
      then slept leaning against them.
In Hell, everything is true.
   *Honeyed twinge / mausoleum.*
      *It's cold* was all we could say for months.
      WITH: THE ABSOLVER.
I am not a newspaperman:
   that is a photograph of my lover in my hatband.
      Nothing is metaphor, one says (staged).
   Nothing is *like* metaphor.
The hose and ice represented by two dancers,
   principles of the thing. We are all sundials, says one.
      One was fresh out. One was a damn sight.
   One could eat you under the table.
In all the photographs, my head flips back.
   I scream when the neighbors do so they think I am watching
      the game.
      I SCREAMED WHEN THE NEIGHBOR WENT INTO LABOR.
   It is a good deal, says one.
A good deal of liquor, says two.
   I'd like one, says one.
      Make that two, says two.
   (One gets one, two: two.)
Or, more real to follow Don Quixote down the lush
   steps as the camera in a film by Bresson
      does not show the face of the ticket-taker
   but only the hero giving his ticket. This is not ego,
as the lens could shift to any face. As tourists recording out a passing
   bus might incidentally catch
      a man pulling out his stitches or live sex.
   *Knight of the Sorrowful.* A CHILD NAMED SORROW.
St. Sebastian: *As every bud to every limb . . .*
   Don Quixote goes to the mechanical chess champion
      now a sushi chef. He orders

the Grand Master Platter, the final moves of
(eating of) which require hours.
    He goes to a druggist and buys some contact solution.
      He asks the believer in the One if Don Quixote exists
enough to have anything, even mono.
Mornings, I limp; you can set your watch by it.
    I wanted to study under you, contracted.
      Bresson's camera fixed on a limb. SORROW.
*I want a human,* said to the airline hotline.
In an empty room, Don Quixote does the imitation of bacon
(lies on the tile; sizzles).
    He puts on some lipstick for the make-up sex.
    Yet: he was most Don Quixote when he was in the audience,
that is, the play was most *Don Quixote*
when it saw Don Quixote in the audience.
    I tape your greeting card to the wall so it is open.
    The student asks, *what do you write when the pain is gone?*
I say, evenly, *there is no pain,* and: *no gone.*
HAVE SOME GUM.
    *Lazy eye / paisley tie.* It is something.
*Translation* is the moving of saints' bones.
"The scarred body versus the victim's cry."
    One cannot be a martyr and endure. *The scarred body verse is.*
    One can remove the bones, or move them inside me.
Doctor: *Point to where it hurts.*
Everywhere I point, therefore, hurts. *Therefore hurts.*
    At parties, I mostly stay awake.
    I see myself telling about the thing I saw.
    Pressing pies to the window for *pines.*
908 WEBSTER STREET, A TYPICAL ADDRESS.
    It is sentimental to think *desire fulfilled is loss* when I want
      you here.
    I press the soft spot (*entrance*) between breast plate and
      throat.
You call that a song?
Everything you've heard is true.
    A French toast dispensing napkin dispenser,
      hammock hitched to fireflies. Sun on a page too bright to read.

To burst: burrs germinate in fur.
One cannot stand beside a windmill without seeming
  to sway with its *tilting at*. Was once in the audience.
    Stage right.
    EXEUNT, WITH FIREFLIES.
*Off stage, a girl pulling leaves from a tree, she*
  *cannot find the right one, keeps pulling, as a rower*
    *pulls beside her on the river (oars lift, dabbling particular*
  *prints briefly in the surface: leaves).*
I tell the students that although I honestly mistook
  the snow for falling blossoms for longer
    than makes sense, I could not write that.
    One leaves crying for his soul.
I was no good with literature, because I thought everything was
    literal:
  it was not a poem about a man who feels like a lion
    in a cage, but about a lion in its cage,
  like a man.
It was not a poem.

When you are locked in a cave, my father taught, close
your eyes and count to seven, so you can see
by contrast with this inner dark.

I close my eyes. I count to seven, higher.

Always putting his hand in the fire
to move a log, and burned, and burned.

He knew the name of everything.

                    Don't open more

than a sleeve button, if you are cold, he said.
You can live your whole life cold.

To touch the seen
  skin as

shelter would,
  mouth of gold leaves

heady and
  unweaning

"I turned the color
  of a man" (Dante)

as though hunger alone
  could outlast one

You were whatever spoke in the dream that was not
my voice or yours. It gave a number, which was how many
years until, or the age we will be when. I said yes and was waking
as in Exodus the wonders are imaged, and quail, yet this Lord is a
    sound.

I bartered until I felt the speech cilia in my throat shudder
even when reading silently, or overheard. The recording
was of the trembling nature makes. They hold up the conductor's
arms because the pose matters, not his still wanting whatever. I
    was just going

to ask whether an approach is always advancing, or if it may
signal moving on as moving through, or even as moving into
an outness. The purpose of time is to slow us. Moses agrees
to receive and then there is this casual everywhere. Disinterested,
    me,

except in what allows, which is sometimes memory and in other
instances requires hoping to see. I sit at the bar until someone
asks me to a table. Wreath-thick hedges. Words to transmit the
    hum.

In the painting by Degas, the dancer is not
on a cell phone, but holding her head. I left the museum.
Ann was sick. There were shoes all along the bridge,
and the senseless branching of ambulance sirens: one going west
on Henderson, another east. Technicolor weather. A man
in white coveralls was carrying a traffic cone
over his head, he was an Elmer's glue tube.
In the painting of terns on rigging,
when you remove the terns from the rigging, there is
only canvas behind, not sky. Ann vomited
off the bridge, the way a single page can slide
from its binding. It became harder for me to read on
in the biography, knowing there is no part of the body
a bullet hasn't pierced. Piercework. I worked in a chowder house
and got to bring home all the innards we extracted
from bread bowls. I had a friend who was a trumpet player
who'd come home from a show and, sleepless, play more.
His apartment was so small, his trumpet
stuck into the alley. Ann slept for two or three months.
Snow like tissue after tissue pulled from a box.
I drove Ann to the hospital. On the first day of spring I saw
the Elmer's man standing on the traffic cone point
of his head at a rave. Trees blossomed outside the hospital
the way champagne bottles christen ships. I wheeled Ann
to the museum and we watched the Indian out front
raise his arms to weather. I talked about the Caravaggios
facing each other in Santa Maria del Popolo, the pose
of Paul, receiving, so close to the pose of Peter,
received; saints open their arms. Pieced through.
My friend the trumpet player emptied his spit valve onto pigeons.
He watched a woman climb onto her fire escape, nude,
her husband cursing from the window. I gave up on
the biography. I left the rave. Ann held her head.
The ambulances were just roaming, moving things around.
I put on some shoes I found on the bridge, then left the bridge.
Ann bruised. Her mom showed up. It was July.

You tell your parents we are getting on.
   Like one's reflection around a missing pane,
      bells do two-thirds of a resolving chord.
   Vendors lift their wares in linens—think
of Cleopatra in her rug—as police
      pace lazily up one end of the alley.
      Let us not be reduced to history.
   Bruno fired near here; near, the Jewish ghetto
where many survived, comparatively.
      Just: cappuccino's gentle bitterness.
      How the foam's holes widen, evidential
      as Caesar's dagger-starred tunic: *here*
*is where one entered* . . .
             We better wrap this up,
      you say. I better let you go. Vendors
      hawk cupid crotch lighters, mechanical bees
      past the cafe rail. Is God obsolete,
a stopped tour guide asks her parasol.
      I hear: *up the sleeve*, like the sudden World
      or Fool a fortune teller scratches out
      existence with. Along these lines: strange grace
of bells that ring with a rag's polishing.

He passed the thermos: pudding in it.
Its lid, now a cup. While we took a break from breaking wreathes
from the hedge.

You know you never fill a tire or basketball when the air is cold,
he said.

      He held me a long time in the cold
to notice things perennial.

## HOTEL

The ledge stops
  somewhat

before the air
  pressed in

its calmed longing
  which feels like snow,

as though a body
  or soul

would have any part
  aside from

aswell

## REAL ESTATE

White trim

    skinnings

in the exterior

    bed under leaves

under snow,

    as the house

siding curls,

    generally speaking

roughed like

    magazine spines

under the end table

    like frescoes

Let us first name
let us first name the quality of forms
commonly known as eternity,
or as close as we can get.

As close as we can get,
we must conscience
our rough knowledge
our rough knowledge of both stone
and the olive

of sun-converting fruit
and a rain-worn wall
on the bare grasses' plain
while marveling, still,

at the convulsed figures passing through
passing through reciting Antony's
*you will be Rome.*

Raked slate
raked slate clouds set a horizon on
on parched marble veins.
Leaves take in wind as though
in wind as though preparing for the fall.

Among so much eternity, we vow.

My love,
nothing is more inhuman than these trees
alive as though excavating up
excavating up into sky,

sharing nothing with our wishes

to claim ourselves
to claim ourselves, in the unchanging,
changed.

Spruce ends near mist along the cross-
sectioned snow's impersonations of scarecrows
stripped by blizzards or folding flannel flap-
arms over dark rodential organs warm in
straw; all morning hand on the burner as
it warms waking you every two minutes
because your loving returning sleep
for a song walking then dogs burrs germinate
in fur and hand purpling at the leash lash
after rabbits all ears in the gathering white
my tracks hem through as a homesteader's
stitch in tulle; I break a swatch of *bittersweet*
the orange berried we summer cut back
from postbox whatever dreamt set in your hand.

cut shades on baking sheets of truck beds. leaf
curls in on self. steam from near brewery
hot off its run-off hits cheeks: turn blushed cough
like I'm the bar stool still, gum carved spun me,
these years I use my body like an oar,
stack cords of quartered storm-fell logs
drive valley ruts check sun-blanched hive doors
(will honey boil?) for Alma old with dogs
on her river bluff. sand bar past the fertile hem
of forest down the field-side bank. scree-slope
for day's sandwiches' sad wishes (mustard salt ham
read dubliners). I slash down new rope
each eve for her so kids don't miss cove swing land
on slants, as water out a hanging plant

Just say the hills are out.
You won't feel a thing.

What we want is really to want.
I have.

Have called this an ending?
A we-can-clean-in-the-morning?

This way you look at me.
It doesn't matter what I've done.

Just say the feeling's been thought.
I have really to want.

(We're trying happiness.
To gain a deeper loss.)

Just drive until you see it.
Just stop.

Do you wanna know what I've done?
You won't feel a thing.

(So an elm leaps over a ditch.
So before all else we seem to have been.)

Because things were better than.
Were better, then.

HELLO

I curse: *O World.*

I sing: *mo-mo, mo-mi, mi-mo.*

*So, song is our only home,*

sang the birds interred

in south-shipped apples, then

in skirt slips warmed.

Sown: field with sweat.

Catching net set over fall.

This second: how much loss

until the first

loss looks like love?

SONG

Sang: present of *wound*

is *wind* (*when*).

Call me: *Man Trying to Unlock*

*Door with Varied Objects.*

*Dramatic Recreation of*

*a Lunar Eclipse.*

Ripest giving gently to a touch

of even frost *tra-la.*

YOU

*Come bail me out,*

sings a canoe to the moon.

You: you train yourself

to reach toward the body

being torn away

by everything that

is tearing you. You leap

until the ground lifts up,

or else you fall to it.

RIDDLE

I am: *Weathervane Lodged*

*Torn in a Farm*

*Hedge at the First Hint*

*of Storm.* The axe handle

splits perfectly.

A man with two rakes

under a magnolia
    rolls his napkin
        into an apple, to ask.
    I take the dead thing to
the compost and sing to it
    for a change.
        SONG
    I sing: *trellis*
*of a crutch.*
    And: *sun like a bell*
        *on a teacher's desk.*
    And: *send me to sea*
*on a piano raft*
    *twist my beard*
        *to straighten my hat*
    *x my eye,*
*x my eye*
    *I steal the sills out*
        *from your pies.*
    PLANTS
I water the plants
    until the ground
        won't hold (a woman
    shreds a quilt
from her balcony, down)
    (the ambulance
        man bends to the man
    in the parking lot's
chest) (calm thumps
    of a child's tethered
        ball). I bend as
    a smoke signal's quilt.
Buds blooming under
    disappear at first
        air but for now
    in my presence opening
as hands releasing arrows.
    GHOST STORY

I recently heard
this charming ghost story:
a mechanical chess champion
at the telephone operator's board.
Call me: *Hopscotch Chalk
Corpse.* I cover
the puddle with my cape
to conceal the lions
therein. I rest under
the pollen-darned
drifts on the windshield
like an action figure
in its case. *Porch screens /
porridge grains. Beaded curtain /
pleated skirt hem.*
SAP
Not a blown kiss:
cigarette drag.
Not a cigarette:
exploding icicle.
I take first watch (*tick*).
Paint myself
into a corner then move
to the walls.
It's full fathom five
below. Breath of autumn air
stuck twixt two winter
panes. Autumn
behind the eyes.
I sing: *I bend to the
hard bead of sap
and breathe.*
REPLY
*Singe here.
Self-clean,* as in, *to burn.
Undetectable repairs*
the mechanic swears by.
*Regrets only*

by the phone number.
    It is a love letter
        because I receive it.
    A love letter
but only I can see it.
    Syllogism: Autumn smells
        like apples. My hands smell
    like woodsmoke/street
ball/leaves.
    My hands must be apples.
        CIRCUS
    I sing: *rest on me*
*like a stretcher.*
    At the *tra-la*
        last moment, a glass
    of *doo-whit* water
appears *fa-fum*
    and the diver lands.
        The first diver
    produces a glass of water
from her sleeve.
    Explicit, if not
        explicable: sun works harder
    to get through now.
Red roof through leaves
    like blossoms in leaves—
        and why not?
    I can't feel it getting colder
yet: June bugs
    overturned on the sidewalk,
        and white.
        BIRD WRIT
The ashes are too large
    for the box.
        Sidecar drives off.
    My tie flips up: black eye.
Hand lifting empty
    of its expected drink, kept

up as a spyglass.
The same waves again are departure.
Right outside the window,
    a man chisels at the window.
        I close the blinds to clean them.
I unfold like a paperclip.
When the door finally unlocks,
    the entire house opens
        but the door stays in place.
    Call me: *Ornithographical.*
*A One-Page Flipbook.*

HOPE

    Or: just to learn
a certain sadness.
Letter says
    *deliver me.* Certainly,
        we babysat
    the potted ferns.
In hanging light.
    Had these envelopes
        licked. Had it out
    out in it. Then struck,
as one would a set.
    Your face was set
        for beauty. Your dresses
    like a felled-tree's leaves.
And: eyes turned up
    like ivy.
        Musing on a hairline cigar.
    Let's go some place
and be quiet.

## FEDERAL CASE

Dark enough

    for hardening

into another,

    which forgives

either the radiant

    tree in a field

or the tree

    in a radiant field

Unblithe,

    the sun harbors

every tatter in

    its assimilating

report:

    hair down a back's

pole

    when not taken advantage of

as though one's practice

    is in question

Of course the dirt that's left is larger than the body.
I washed until there was blood, then until the blood was gone.
Shadows of clouds marked the field
like marker rocks we got from the field.
I am implying that clouds somehow become stones,
it is part of a cycle, we harvest. I mean
I stood at the window, my breath obstructing my eyes,
then wiped the clouds off. Of course I anticipated
the smell. When you decide to finally appear
behind me naked as morning snow,
please understand, whatever you're asking, yes.

I don't know if your window was dark this morning
when I checked walking to school
or if I was just seeing soil through the glass. Wait,
the window was ice, I remember back in fall
when I was switching screens for storm panes
and this moment when I couldn't tell
if a frame held x or y and I knew I'd have to wait
until winter to find out. We were never that intimate,
though I find myself holding you similarly:
is it my fault the only word I remember in Hebrew
is land?

chipped toenail painted sun I strung a fence
along it raced so when I bent it dove
through posts. duck blind I watch ducklings mince
in eddies stuttering sprinkler heads. white crow
I swear as though was never changed gives glance
at me like vestal virgins would to spare
condemned men. can only come by chance,
will be looked into. the knot barbs glare
as cells of blackberries I reach thorned into
or better smelt-lined tide peaks I drive by
home to a steaming field. I think of you
when stars point to me I still identify
imagining your pointing heel. what myth
means more than this is how we've come to this

The building wears dusk
like cut-off jeans. Pretty
girl like you. Bulletproof. I
remember love: the slur
of someone yelling passing
very quickly. Passion. Is it easiest
to love a realist? Isn't everything
realism? Or, the music
must be all around for us
to hear it? A crisis averts only
toward crisis? The kind of movie
you'll watch on cable but
never rent? To hitchhike, the eye
rounds itself. They keep
a moving van on hand here. Smoke
is a smock. Clams, clamps.
What a good idea, these clams.
And the philharmonic conductor
guiding planes to land. Only
be memorable. I reply short
and deep, a man. The mailbox
puts on its rosebush, dawn.
Sap is the neon of trees.

I wake and whatever my pants, backpack, all of the things

necessary are in their pockets. Clean-cut, light switch, there is a
    mirror
on the door's back perhaps one witnessed alterations executed in
    on entering?

Young fawn limbs, I wake, mind tires in mud, unfolding

to purchase one unnecessarily cold green soda, yield, my legs
moving under me as for many years they have bodily through
invoices of rain. I am massive and straught, floodlit, requested

for the proper verb: my final memory of the last thing

I wanted among exquisite forking and strains, Prague stronghold

zoo for bats, was after even my friends had slouched
and boxed themselves, partial and unstaved, holding my entirety

by a finger I ran along this other's lobby embankment
of mailboxes until your name, a nail, and somehow railing

myself upwards, staircases, and I do not know what

I should apologize for, or revolvings extensively glimpsed

friend even now in me as a kettle on the um of some accreting,
    glacial blaze.

## ANIMAL

I wash everything on as hot as it can be. My old towel

still hangs by the bath, never drying. The steam itself
is a shower curtain, and my sweat presses back as fast as I wash
    —this body's

a *waste*, as in, plain, an *expanse*, yet I feel such a pleasant
    strumming in my personal

surfaces, our ongoing passionate disaster, these meanings that
    rub one foot
against its other three times unavoidably at the instant

directly abutting dozing, of long legs and a low fence, and one
    thing always

staying behind to leave, so therefore we are not the problem.

I know all prayers should end in fire or a river, and everything I
    say begins
with its hortation implied: I like that the word itself means *let us*
and that it appears tied to *hours* and *ahora*, *now*, therefore,
*aloha*, and: *alors*. The allurements of these features uphold me,
days we have spent fixing fences that, in Jill's phrase,
*lean now like old dogs*, (I see them, and *now*, as actually leaning *in*
her phrase, voice, situated extant there), as these days themselves
    begun certainly

coming together in exhaustion, once we have worked in sun

and swum in the pond, and imagined at once, aloud, so to speak,
as you were saying, you get my drift, you're telling me.

thistle blur and plant called you say hen and chicks.
we've been arguing about life's busyness,
how the perfect conditions might yet fix
us beside such water skimmers' creeks yet. this
two by two with friends down slopes silences
us we make up quiet touch as a felled log for
a bridge. flat vole on trail. a painted sense
of being among expanses we'll call cures
snuck off among reeds later. still, one needs
more work: let us. a dog shakes at command,
you, arrived from where, nap or, dozing, read
head to key spot my ribs meet. a crissing dam
of bleached trunks newspaper box nets half a boat
pile as we go on, dear time-breathed freckled throat

Then I was as happy
as a hot air balloon
in a ham sandwich.
Healing thinned me.
I no longer scuffed
steps' rubber no-trip
strips. I chose regret
again. Again again.
Then I was great ape sad.
Could hardly hoist my wind-
skinned eyes. Veined sight.
Blight. All things being two
colliding. I was one: none,
elided. The ballerina leaves
didn't spin. Rabbits puked.
Whole zones snowed. Then
light on water, yes.
Cathedral cone green
rhymed to sky. Each look,
a lip to kiss. "It's six
p.m. on Saturday
and I am calling you!"
I slept inside a duck.
You touched my touch. Then a breeze
seeded me. I learned
my lesion. A plane
unzipped the nightsky's fly.
Then northern lights. Each glimpse,
a spritz. Then igloo eyes.
Asshole eyes! Each inch, an itch.
Then fray, and fray, and fray.

## SIDEWALK SALE

As far as things

    handling themselves,

emphatically,

    as a figure

of speaking tends

    to the transitional

among others,

    an ache more

than ever

    regardless

so that sexual

    hunger, we have been told,

will increase

    thresholds

## BLACK WALNUT ADORATION

cue stick horizon. a wrap around. I hold
up my end of the window setting. Jim nails.
sawdust my nose, ancient plain's smoke gold
distance hints at dock kids shooting seals,
half-dollar fields knot-hole swirled in wind,
tv antennae plume of a blue whale.
we paint what we can't mend: curled shingles blend
with scab grass, barrow's tar strips—abruptly pale,
Jim yelps stiff one arm hangs I don't let go
fifty pound sill and frame over him, he hits
dead limb with elbow catch on siding, blood flows—
and suffering? Jim: quota will be met.
forget it. dusk—a primer—has, hushed, vowed:
smell of black walnuts crushed on the road

# FOOL

PLAINS
    Let's to the mountains.
        I see plains in your eyes.
    Cigarette butts
in the rainwater jar
    like pickled grubs.
        I traced the spring with a dye
    made of peaches.
Painted carrier pigeons
    to the walls.
        Then flagged down a dramatic
    score. What am I?
I am made of feelings
    and toys.
        I throw the toy then run.
    I have feelings all the time.
To show how large
    my feeling is
        I'll put one hand here, then run.
BERRIES
The berries
    want us to squish them!
        I sing: *sun strapped*
*to the tracks*
*like a Christmas penny.*
    What falls and isn't
        hurt? Snow.
    *Closing your eyes*
*in a claustrophobic room*
    *should be no different*
        *from closing your eyes*
    *in a meadow.*
I halve this peppermint,
    and the northern lights.
        I make a thousand
    tiny snow angels
with this corkscrew.
    I sleep with my belly

to her back like I'm holding
in a wound.
BEASTS
   I let you walk along
      the curb, being more concerned
  with cars out of storefronts.
A man becomes
   an undertaker because he cannot
      afford flowers. A girl
  reading a book soaked
by rain reaches out
   her hand to feel for rain.
      I whisper *timber*.
  I whisper *fall*.
I climb the trees and feel
   for fruit with my boots.
      Every beast is afraid
  of some other beast.
If you keep enough
   beasts around you,
      all the beasts will stay away.
   PLEASANTNESS AND SHAME
I touch each stair
   first with my face.
      Hold myself
  by a single finger up
against the mailboxes'
   names. I keep lifting
      the mailbox's
  flag so the postman
will grasp inside.
   I warm my hands
      on the burner.
  Post-it Notes stuck
to the wall and the wall
   demolished. Do the Dutch
      inhale (like a windmill).
  Do the Corsican

shuffle (*you shuffle*).
    I move the circle
        (miner's headlamp)
    on my brow down
for a monocle.
      DUMB FATE
      It's just dumb fate.
    *Well All Is Hope.*
Diacritical clouds
    on imaginary bluffs.
      I am in this desert
    standing on this stepladder
just being Jesus
    holding up
      some aluminum siding
    *when.*
I perfected the surgery
    with a kite.
      I lie like bagged leaves heaped
    in a rubbish strike.
*Panic Whimsies,*
    I name the sled dogs.
      *Reality Epistles,*
    I call the sandbox toads.
SONG
    Sang: *book upside-down*
      *turn your glasses around*
    *and cut off your nose if they're scissors!*
I blow my nose on a hill.
    I stand like this
      so I appear to be running.
    At the airport, I will be the one
wearing an airport.
    Sun face down like a magazine.
      PARADE
    At the airport,
I will use the artificial
    tree as a terrorist would.

Loose tobacco on the tongue
like pubes.
Loose thermometer mercury
like Monopoly hotels.
I would take you in
my arms, as one takes in
lawn furniture.
Flinching at birds
as candy thrown.
Cardinals stapled
to a float's crepe.
Your eyes the only stationary parts.
AUBADE
I exhaust myself
painting *wet paint*
continuously
on the cans of housepaint.
*Shh,* goes the twist
on the bread loaf bag.
Your breath
like boots
through plasticky snow.
Bubble gum pops:
surgical mask.
Kissing sounds compose
the neighborhood dogs.
Why take a picture
of something that already exists?
SUN
Sun on my chest
like a permission slip
taped to a child.
I am so small
I lean back to open doors.
So many things
I'll never lift.
I'd shake your hand
but my knuckles crack.

In my urban camouflage:
white jumpsuit
with a gumball machine
painted on.
I watch you sleep
like a dark age man guarding
a cave painting giraffe.
I momentarily forget my stitches
and smile.

DREAM

Scarecrow folds
his arms over
some burrowed squirrel
heart. The giant
human bunny
unzips its suit and
a small real bunny
is inside.
Why? *I wanted there*
*to be some mystery,* he says.
I pour as much milk
as I will need
onto my cereal then pour
it back into the jug
then pour out the rest
of the jug.
I sing: *digital clock*
*giving chapter and verse.*

LIMP

Dad, I have a limp.
Just walk it off.
Clouds as empty
finger casts.
Egg carton clouds.
*If song be sung enough . . .*
*If sung song be enough . . .*
I wash my mouth out
with sugar.

It widows me.
    Trying to get full
        on sugar packs alone.
    Scene: a parting shot.
A crawl through a cannon.
    Yawning in my sleep.
       SONG
    Sang: *birds like tire*
*scraps along*
    *an interstate.*
        Our gang: the snapdragons.
    In winter light
like snap peas
    I suck the cold air in
        to soothe my gums.
    I tunnel out.
As long as I never come up,
    I will be free.
        As one who cannot flee
    yet flies.
It doesn't matter.
    You can say anything you have to.
       EPIC
    The hero sits
and you realize he
    has been traveling all this time
        with a shot leg.
    An untrained voice passes.
It is passable.
    Your migraine,
        with rainfall.
    My weathering, in dandelions.
Remember, there was
    this fountain when you turned
        to it it
    stopped you shook your head
to remember your earrings
    I closed my eyes

and it began again.

GOODBYE

Dear complex of simple
    through-skin
        breath, I do not believe
    we were thinking
the same song.
    The one that goes
        *ship, come in.*
    That one that goes
*under braising stars.*
    That goes
        *you can spend your whole life cold.*
    What am I?
I'll play this piano
    with a rake.
        And sing: *and muscle through.*
    And I'll sing out: *trellis of a crutch.*

## ON A POSE OF VIRGIL'S

Near its peak, the mountain requires nearly no
effort to climb. There is no sky behind the flags,
barges of pretty silt. Some wrestlers oil themselves
to prevent a grip, others rub grit on their skin

to help it. In the cartoon, Orpheus puts glasses on the back
of his head and walks in reverse. The pastor's white
collar is a foam neck brace. I am sorry to hear,
this morning, as I can't see the mug top through

the pouring steam, that there is nothing new in
philosophy: I meant to tell you a story but cannot
keep myself interested long enough to describe
the pinewoods exactly. I can never remember jokes,

but there were twenty-four flavors of syrup for
the soft-serve, as for an entire day of ice cream,
and a man near the summit holding his palms fast to
the grass, waiting for dew to come so he could wash.

## POEM FOR MY WIFE IF WE ARE MARRIED

I.

I have told you before my recurring dream.
A man drives to a field where his house once was.
He stands like a scarecrow, where the backyard was.
Now: nature is as it is when it has its way.
(If winter had one choice, it would kill us, our friend
Andy wrote.) His white work shirt in, say, sun-
Light looks like the makeshift bedsheet screen once
Hung alder to elm and fertilized with beams square from
A projector on a pick-up's rippled bed. His parents,
Aunts, the woman down the road whose mailbox's flag
Would sit up daily months after she died, as though
To coax the postman to grasp inside and dirty
His uniform, maybe the elementary school music teacher
Who brought the folding chairs, with moons
Of paper plates printed with pie stains on
Their laps . . . He explains: the screen, its sheet, was old.
So, it had holes. From fever, bleach. So pieces of film
Pressed through to salt the ground below. Behind
The screen—they crawled, he and the cousin who threatened,
Once, to tear off his balls, and the cousin
He wrestled with where the river moved just enough
To hold you still as you thrashed. Later, he will drive
A thresher these cousins walk along beside loading
Tassels through its arms. Now, they are mad
To have the bits of movie on their skin. Part of a car chase,
Inch of ocean, pinch of a face. On his cousin's throat
Like a bow. A crisp flake on his tongue (did I catch one?)
Where the film slips through—having opened his shirt,
He touches his chest. Here, and here, and here.

2.

I don't know what it means. A patch of ladder leans against
A pane. The drama of a leaf caught in a web, spinning so its
   binds
Are visible. I don't know any more than light against a pane.
Kevin said: It sounds like a post-modern Plato's cave. So,
   salvation's
Fleeing? Or, can we press in—to the distilled air—and thus
Press save? How much I'd like to only list the world for you,
To say reality, though we are in it, is what we want, because,
While we are in it, we still find it wanting. That art can make
The grass I described as *salted* more grass if its depiction is
Vaulted by buttresses of fertilizing style, which we don't need
Because of a lived loss of sense, but because of how much grass
   even
Imagined grass around us is. And: that *can*, in art, thus love, is
   *should.*
I am driving through rain to you. Umbrellas broken near curbs
Like salmon I saw in Olympia, Washington, growing up that
   swam
Up through storm drains. They shone along the sidewalks when
I reached toward them. A salmon, one knows, is made
To leap against a dam. I wanted to write you a poem made of
Solidities that would leap like that, not only to speak a known
Note but to prove notes multiply in instruments—like that
   dragonfly
We found, once, like paper splayed beneath our wiper blade: that
   was
Our ticket? I want to prove the world is beautiful because
We are only in it. The way I am continually startled but not
   surprised
To see that you are beautiful. I need to keep blinking. And there
   you are:
Standing, skin mixing warm damp, a novel by Henry James, with
Me in the car. (I like Roman spolia, you know, more than mosaic
Or collage—the way the face of Aphrodite sits among other

Discarded rubble used for bricks. Her purpose is not to be
    defamiliarized
To shock like a shovel on an art house wall, but, simply: a brick.
And yet—you sit close to me, best part of my day—there is
The face of Aphrodite, like a pure rhyme inside a discrete
    strophe.)

3.

I cannot see what flowers.
You are a window-toucher. You point, holding me,
So I am pointing. What image is not contemporary
Before us? My dream's? A nipple through some clothes.
This is the thesis? "Fragments do not juxtapose
But expose wholeness; fragments show life's fullness . . ."
In Rome while I taught you wandered looking for a hat
To point out to me later. Our apartment full
Of decorative straw hats and rifles mounted on the wall
Was above a welder's shop. Watering the plants I'd pour
Water through dry soil so it pooled beneath the orange-
Edged flames. A man would crane up at me from the shape—
Me-shaped?—I had made. His shop was called (translation,
    please)
Mr. Joining's. You said, laughing (I joined in): Don't tell me we're
Above a pun! One wants all meanings to split perfectly,
As distinct as an angel made of chairs, a vase you see
And then see cracked, and then see has been for a long
Time healed. Am I still seeing you? Lucas asked last week.
I burrow in. On you like a dog with its chew toy. Squeak.
Sweats salt your back, upper lip. "All things counter,
Original, spare, strange"—first lines I ever learned.

4.

I want to prove the world is beautiful. And then?
To prove it is not from a collapsing need
That looks away toward simple truths to prove
There is nothing but admiring that we can do.
I want the black water through the dock slats, nails
Bending like a spine across them, some original stoner's
Marker message unknowingly echoing a Merwin line
I memorized to tell a girl you would have seen through.
Does this have anything to do with you? Is there
Anything less personal than love? A beggar grabs your belt—
It has nothing to do with you—you could be anyone—
Yet, as from the locative obliterative principle
Of a tromp l'oeil's direct address—now you have
A beggar on your belt. We read to find out what
We love, says Thomas Lux. My story of reading is
I will soon leave to meet you. Can art match this?
I love: not the world turned to, always, but, always,
The turn itself, which makes Wordsworth talk straight—
Better than the talking straight?—the moment one
Decides to start a band—so much better than
Song—how modernism comes smuggled in a peg leg on sail
    cloth
To a continent. Public library I spent school lunches at
As though a book could save me. We reel in.
Kite-world: world turns, as at dawn's clawing through
The mini-blinds, you turn. To me? For some other darkness
At which we'll close our eyes? Those Merwin lines? Roughly:
From all the ages how little has come to me that is
Breath and nothing that is you. I can't hear now where
They end. I call the ending beautiful.

My barber at the ocean was a surfer, he gazed past my cowlick to the drugstore like it was ocean. I arrived early to the carousel mall where my lover worked to see the Chinese restaurant owners' daughter, Sally, ride her while she mopped. We walked home along the river. My lover's boyfriend carried the bed with me up the stairs, I was on the downside. Days later, in the apartment we moved to when we got back from the ocean, my lover bought a bed we assembled sitting in the middle of the frame. We were broken up by then, because of my lover who I sat with cherry blossoms around us like camera flashes and the Japanese picnickers. She moved a chair near the couch to keep yelling at me when I moved to the couch to sleep. I tried to move to Boston to be with my I-hoped-lover whose name meant apricot but she tore apart a red pepper with her hands and went to Japan to do art. My lover the art student had me pose with the dead birds I broke up with her on her twenty-third birthday. I lived alone and juggled three hours a day. My lover took me to the cabin her father the pilot flew over and I pretended to sleep. When we lived together we slept on a mattress on the floor, a boat, in a car. We thought the condensation dripping from the window was sweat. I went to Italy and she told me when she was in the Israeli army on the Lebanese border there was a tree she would visit at night. She piled rocks on my body as a woman had to her in the desert and I felt only her hand. I went back to the city and my lovers got me high on a driveway and told me to go. I received a letter and didn't respond. I actually mailed rose petals. "I turned the color of a man," Dante says. Her parents had one TV for sound, one for picture, and now her mom has cancer. She told me to survive you are careful where you go, and you have luck. She wrote me an email after two years. She told me I had been simply forgotten. "I thought you were a man of integrity," my best friend said. Often, I'd wake to her pacing a cramp from her foot, on the rug like the sound in a shell. We disconnected the smoke alarm before cooking fish sticks. I called her the wrong name. I watched her tape her breasts for the backless, and zipped her. The mirror went from skin to black. I came too fast. Then we left the high school, my hands already in her. The penis scabbed. I plucked a hair from her nipple, and promised.

## OF CONVENIENCES

We both

    have different views

(not enough

    to place my hand

in the hole

    where the hymnal

goes

    under the undoing

bulbs)

A correcting

    vault, arch

and the choir's

    ribs, skirting inter-

laced

    and the letting of hills

do the work for us,

    we are

after a fashion

    taken up

as the shadow which is

    branch's limit

It is 1970. My father, the drop out,
has been hired to run a push-mower over the southern field.
The other laborers will leave at lunch to float
in the quarry pool. So, alone, he will peel
plastic party cups from the open blades.
He is wondering about hitchhiking home
to Detroit, where my mother, a motel maid,
naps on the clock. Dust from a gopher's mound. Hen-
white sun. (The story is, my grandfather
was captured when his plane became a wave.
He died years later.) John has yet to hear
the record he will buy tonight and tape
to mail my mother. I have it playing now.
Its vinyl's palm lines click, like weeds in a plow.

Because one

   unpixeled

part of the screen or

   projection

does not hue

   except as a perfect

white nub that one,

   filmed,

at times grazes

   or dilates around

as the winded

   blooms one thought first

bees

## SEE THROUGH

Brimful, as
    a planetarium

the space inside
    equivalent

to all around,
    like us, Rome wasn't

built, you said,
    its countryside just

gave up around it,
    as a fountain's pool

brimming so steadily,
    it stills

## WHY LIE

Scatter on grass of seed sparrows
took from the grain cache,
catch in my throat, catch in the checked

axe latched locked in the chop block:

could a map in alfalfa or flax lift
the shape of the noon
birds' chase up from the storm-
flat glade (a claptrap of matchsticks
spun to its sides like shirts
in a washer) as a sign

sure as the sap on my denim back
where I leaned—gleaned:

boot-braced, brought the blade back
from the stump, stamped, stamped,
paid, to work. I'd give my arms, though,
or claim my heart goes out,
to hash up one last crust of name

for a just, unclever mutterance:

when she shook her head the windmills hushed;
mine was lust.

## A DEDICATION

I have a scratch on the surface of my eye
like the visible inch of a web
among a barn's competing drafts and light.

I have heard early astronomers denounced
whole centuries after spying canals
etched in Martian passes cataracting
like Oriental characters across
a gaseous lens. They imagined boating there
like you did in the Borghese that day I slept.
Oar scar on lake. A duckling's trace.

Later, among the interminable picturesque
nineteenth-century scenes, I turned to face
a shiver near a saint with frogs for hands.
His tongue? I blinked. It wasn't there. It was
*in* my sight, like an oven's pilot light.

It is like the line a stump's lines start from.
It is a fence wire so sharp who needs barbs.

When I breathe out hard, it shakes. Are we dancing yet?
You hold this scrape like you're helping a toddler. I have
so little, love, not even chisel or rock
I could fashion a fountain from one night
below your window. I feel it would keep you up,
but the secret of poetry is cruelty,
said a poet who used to live in our town,
but I would rather sleep inside with you.

What more does love come to than that? It comes
to this: I use up the water in my squirting flower
and hand you the flower. Here is a shell large enough
to hold whatever ocean. All for one,
for you: an hourglass tapped, its sap coagulates.
For you. For all love is dedicates.

The title of this collection comes from Jon Kabat-Zinn's guide to mindfulness and healing of the same name. I used to attend poetry readings at Prairie Lights Books in Iowa City. Kabat-Zinn's book was often on a shelf near the reader's head, like a caption. I love the phrase—how *full* is the catastrophe, how *full* is the living that follows.

The figure, Frost says, is the same for poetry as for love. If the most meaningful is possible, why do anything else?

I owe huge thank yous to all of the friends who have supported me and these poems, especially Jay Thompson, Melissa Dickey, Andy Stallings ("so burn is slow—so what?"), Sam Reed, and Meg Schäfer. I'm grateful also to Dorothy and Marvin Bell, David Hamilton, Dean Young, Cole Swensen, Jim Galvin, Linda Bierds, Mary Ruefle, Connie Brothers, the Iowa Writers' Workshop, Kenyon College, and the International Institute of Modern Letters in Wellington, New Zealand. Also, for conversation that inflected these poems, to Dora Malech, Mark Leidner, Dan Rosenberg, Isaac Sullivan, Caryl Pagel, Danny Khalastchi, Cassie Donish, Kat Factor, Tyler Meier, G. C. Waldrep, Mo Brown, Kevin Craft, Kaethe Schwehn, Lauren Haldeman, and Steve Dold. Holly Carver and the University of Iowa Press have been everything I've dreamed of for this book. Richard Kenney and the University of Washington's Creative Writing Seminar in Rome showed me a room engineered so when you stand on a tiled globe and clap, an echo ricochets exactingly down your scalp; they showed me life like that.

Lastly, thank you to my parents, Kathy and John Savich.

1987
Elton Glaser, *Tropical Depressions*
Michael Pettit, *Cardinal Points*

1988
Bill Knott, *Outremer*
Mary Ruefle, *The Adamant*

1989
Conrad Hilberry, *Sorting the Smoke*
Terese Svoboda, *Laughing Africa*

1990
Philip Dacey, *Night Shift at the
  Crucifix Factory*
Lynda Hull, *Star Ledger*

1991
Greg Pape, *Sunflower Facing the Sun*
Walter Pavlich, *Running near the
  End of the World*

1992
Lola Haskins, *Hunger*
Katherine Soniat, *A Shared Life*

1993
Tom Andrews, *The Hemophiliac's
  Motorcycle*
Michael Heffernan, *Love's Answer*
John Wood, *In Primary Light*

1994
James McKean, *Tree of Heaven*
Bin Ramke, *Massacre of the
  Innocents*
Ed Roberson, *Voices Cast Out to
  Talk Us In*

1995
Ralph Burns, *Swamp Candles*
Maureen Seaton, *Furious Cooking*

1996
Pamela Alexander, *Inland*
Gary Gildner, *The Bunker in the
  Parsley Fields*
John Wood, *The Gates of the Elect
  Kingdom*

1997
Brendan Galvin, *Hotel Malabar*
Leslie Ullman, *Slow Work through
  Sand*

1998
Kathleen Peirce, *The Oval Hour*
Bin Ramke, *Wake*
Cole Swensen, *Try*

1999
Larissa Szporluk, *Isolato*
Liz Waldner, *A Point Is That Which
  Has No Part*

2000
Mary Leader, *The Penultimate Suitor*

2001
Joanna Goodman, *Trace of One*
Karen Volkman, *Spar*

2002
Lesle Lewis, *Small Boat*
Peter Jay Shippy, *Thieves' Latin*